THE ART OF KNITTING

Most women learn how to knit and for many it is an absorbing and enjoyable occupation which results in individually styled garments for the family to wear. Hand knitting is supplemented by an extensive industry producing a wide range of knitted garments, and it is with the development of the machine knitting industry that this book is concerned.

Knitted fabric differs from woven fabric in that it does not have a separate warp and weft but is composed of a regular series of interlocking loops made from one continuous thread. This gives it a much greater elasticity than woven fabric, so that it moulds more readily to the shape of the human body and is therefore particularly useful for closely fitting garments such as stockings, socks and vests. It is, however, not easy to make good knitted fabric; the yarn has to be even and well twisted, with no thin places which could result in a broken thread, while the loops need to be of the same size and locked together. A broken thread or dropped loop can result in the whole garment unravelling.

It is perhaps for these reasons that woven fabric seems to have been made earlier than knitted fabric, despite the need for a piece of fixed equipment such as a loom. The first kind of knitting was probably similar to the French knitting that children still do using pins stuck into a cotton reel. Loops were formed round pegs stuck into a rectangular or circular frame and then a second series of loops was wound round. The first series could be drawn over the second series by the fingers or a hooked implement like a crochet hook. This method produces a tube of fabric similar to that made using three or four needles, which seems to have been the way in which knitting with straight needles developed. Certainly by the fifteenth century caps and stockings were being made in Britain using needles rather than a peg frame.

In hand knitting one needle is kept rigid and holds the knitting previously completed, while new loops are created and drawn through the loops on the rigid needle by a second needle which is moved to and fro. The first knitting machine or *stocking frame,* invented in 1589 by a Nottinghamshire clergyman called William Lee, was based upon the principle of a fixed needle with a second moving one which formed the loops and drew them through the set of loops last made. As with other inventions for textile manufacture, such as the spinning jenny, Lee was concerned to replace the one implement wielded by the hand worker

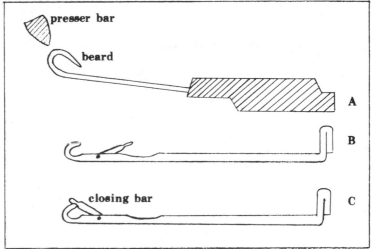

A bearded needle (A) with the pointed end bent into a loop which can be closed by means of the presser bar. On the latch needle (B and C) the hinged pin closes the loop when it is pushed across by the yarn travelling up the stem of the needle.

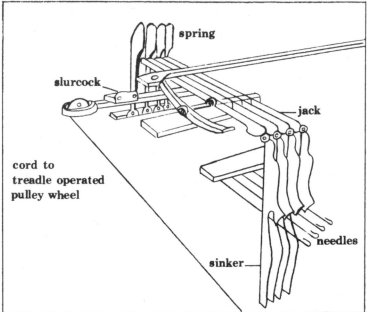

spring

slurcock

jack

cord to
treadle operated
pulley wheel

needles

sinker

Part of the knitting frame mechanism. The cord from the pulley wheel moves the slurcock along a bar, which pushes the springs backwards. The jacks, which are pivoted in the centre, are thus released and allow the sinkers to drop between the needles.

— in this case a needle — by a number of them so that the fabric could be produced more quickly. The rigid needles in Lee's machine had long stems with the pointed ends bent backwards into hooks. This *bearded needle* was his solution to the problem of drawing a new loop of yarn through loops previously made without dropping them. The beard or hooked part of the needle could be pressed into a groove in the stem of the needle, so enclosing a row of new loops. The old loops supporting the fabric already knitted could be drawn forward over the closed beard so that they slipped down to hang on the new loops contained in the beard. This type of needle continued to be used in machine knitting until it was partly superseded by the *latch needle,* similar to a rug hook, during the nineteenth century.

Lee's equivalent of the moving needle which made and transferred the loops was small metal plates, called *sinkers,* hanging vertically between the needles. These were attached at the top to levers or *jacks,* which were pivoted in the centre. The weight of the sinkers would tilt the jacks, and so the free end of each jack was held in position by a notched

spring. A locker bar kept them all in place, but they were released when required by a small piece of metal, the *slurcock,* which travelled along a bar underneath the springs and released each jack one by one. The slurcock was controlled by a cord passing round a central pulley and could be made to move left or right by the two outer treadles on the machine. A thread was laid across the stems of the needles and by means of one of the treadles the jacks were released and the *jack sinkers* fell one by one between every two needles and so made the loops in sequence, pulling in extra thread from the free end. If all the jack sinkers came down at once, the strain would have been too great on the thread and it would be broken. The loops were even because the jack sinkers were carefully adjusted so that each came down exactly the same distance. Lee's original machine could produce only a coarse fabric, but his brother later added a second series of sinkers, the *lead sinkers,* which were fixed to a bar and came down all at once between the jack sinkers, forming a loop over every needle, and so creating a finer fabric than could be produced on the original machine. The

ABOVE: *The birthplace of the framework knitting industry: Calverton, Nottinghamshire. Windles Square, built in 1834, originally formed part of a group of twenty-two houses around three sides of a square. Now there remains only an L-shaped terrace, which was restored between 1972 and 1974 by the Nottinghamshire Buildings Preservation Trust. The long windows typical of stockingers' shops can be seen on the ground floor. The large gardens were a more unusual feature.*

COVER: *A watercolour painting of Jeff Oxley, who at the age of seventy-nine was still working a hand frame. By permission of G. H. Hurt and Son, Chilwell, Nottinghamshire.*

FRAMEWORK KNITTING

Marilyn Palmer

Shire Publications Ltd

CONTENTS

Set in 9 point Times and printed in Great Britain by C. I. Thomas & Sons (Haverfordwest) Ltd, Press Buildings, Merlins Bridge, Haverfordwest, Dyfed SA61 1XE.

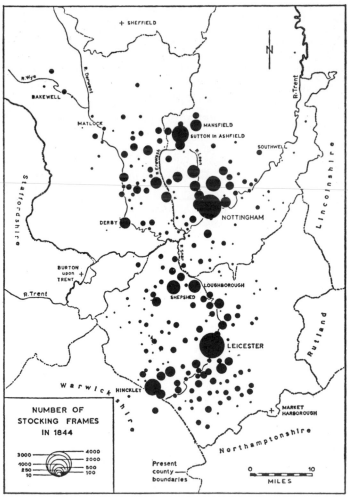

The distribution of stocking frames in the East Midlands, based on information given in the 1844 Framework Knitters' Report. Notice the concentration along the valleys of the Soar, Trent, Leen and Erewash rivers, and the way in which satellite villages are clustered around the main distribution centres of Leicester, Loughborough, Nottingham and Sutton in Ashfield.

sinkers were carefully shaped to perform a second task, that of pushing the loops backwards and forwards on the stem of the needle, and so they were in every way the equivalent of the hand knitter's moving needle.

The sequence of working a stocking frame can be followed by means of the diagrams. The knitter first lays a thread across the stems of the needles, either by hand or with a mechanical device known as a *thread carrier* (A). Pressing down one of the outer treadles with his foot, he releases the slurcock and so causes the jack sinkers to fall one by one between every two needles to form the loops (B). He then pushes with both hands on the thumb plates at each end of the carriage and releases the sinker bar, bringing down the lead sinkers to divide the loops already made : the jack sinkers rise slightly at the same time to equalise the loops (C). With his hands the knitter then pulls forward the carriage so that the sinkers push the new loops forward under the needle beards, the old loops being held under the arches of the sinkers (D). The carriage is then lifted to remove the

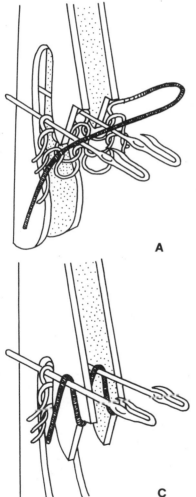

A

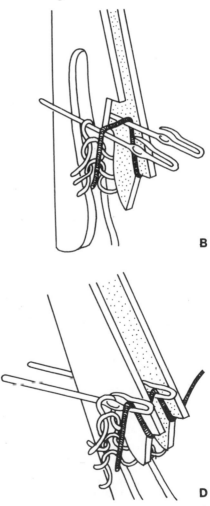

B

C

D

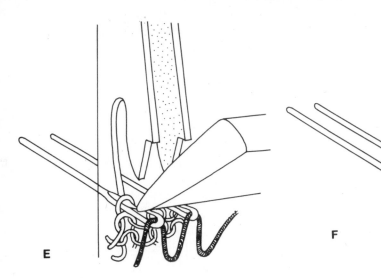

E

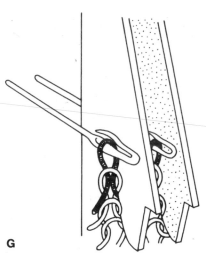

F

sinkers from between the needles. The knitter then depresses the central treadle with his foot, thus bringing a presser bar down on the needle beards and closing them (E). The carriage is then pulled forward so that the long jack sinkers push the old loops on to the needle beards. He then removes his foot from the middle treadle to release the presser bar and pulls the carriage fully forwards to knock the old loops over the closed beards so that they slip off and hang over the new loops inside the needle beards (F). Using one of the outer treadles, the knitter releases the jacks again so that the arches of the sinkers can take the fabric back up the stems of the needles as the carriage is pushed backwards (G). When the jacks are raised again, another row of loops can be made and the sequence repeated.

Working the stocking frame required considerable physical effort, both from the hands and arms in moving the carriage and from the feet and legs in working the treadles. Good sight was also needed as the machine required frequent adjustment. It could only produce a flat piece of material, not a tube of fabric, but by increasing or decreasing the number of loops made it was possible to widen or narrow the fabric to follow, for example, the shape of the leg. This was then taken off the frame and seamed up, forming a

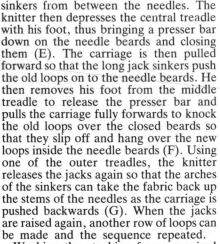

G

fully fashioned stocking. Women usually undertook the seaming, while because of the strenuous exertion required working the frame was usually the man's job. Children or women wound the thread from hanks on to bobbins. Framework knitting, as it came to be called, was therefore an occupation in which all the family participated and one which could be carried out at home since only muscle power was needed.

Working a hand frame was a strenuous occupation. The knitter used both feet to operate the treadles and both arms to move the heavy iron carriage on its wooden frame. To the left of the frame is a floor vice and to the right a bobbin winder, adapted from an old spinning wheel: these were used to transfer yarn from hanks to bobbins for use on the frame.

ABOVE: *The knitting frame with the presser bar in position to close the needle beards. The most recently formed row of loops can be seen hanging in the beards. The vertical plates behind the presser bar are the sinkers.*

LEFT: *Richard Sackville, Earl of Dorset, in 1616. Fashion decreed that much of the leg was on display. This stimulated the production of knitted silk hose, often embroidered like this example.*

8

Apprentices were trained in framework knitting for a period of seven years. This indenture, dated November 1753, binds Joseph Shardlow apprentice to Henry Marshall, a framework knitter of the parish of St Alkmund's, Derby.

THE GROWTH OF FRAMEWORK KNITTING

Hand knitting probably developed as an industry rather than a domestic employment in Britain during the fifteenth century, when the woollen industry was expanding rapidly. Acts of Parliament concerning clothing refer to knitted woollen caps, while household books mention knitted hose. The demand for these had been created by a change in fashion. The long robes worn by men were beginning to be replaced by doublets and short trunks and so the legs and the hose which covered them were on display. Previously hose had been cut from woven cloth, possibly on the bias, and then seamed from toe to welt. While warm enough, it was not very sightly as it did not mould itself to the shape of the wearer. The wealthy began to purchase knitted silk stockings, at first from Spain and Italy, but then from English suppliers during the sixteenth century. These were often elaborately embroidered, particularly in the section above the ankle known as the clox. It is said that when Queen Elizabeth I's silk woman, Mrs Montague, presented her mistress with a pair of knitted black silk stockings the Queen resolved never to wear cloth hose again.

Hand knitting flourished to meet the new demand, particularly as a secondary employment in rural areas where wages were low and additional income was needed. It may have been concern for his poverty-stricken parishioners which stimulated the Reverend William Lee, curate of Calverton in Nottinghamshire, to invent the stocking frame in 1589. The story is generally told that Lee was courting a young lady, who, when he visited her, concentrated on her knitting and ignored the advances of her admirer. He therefore determined to invent a machine which would supersede this absorbing female occupation. It is more probable that he was just fascinated by the technical problems of mechanising so complex a process as knitting, as a clergyman of a later period, Edmund Cartwright, inventor of the power loom, was with weaving.

Lee's parishioners evidently regarded his machine as a threat rather than an adjunct to their employment, for Lee left Calverton and took his stocking frame to London, where he tried to interest Queen Elizabeth I in his invention. He was unsuccessful because his machine, equipped only with jack sinkers, could not produce so fine a fabric as the royal hand knitters. The government anyway was unwilling to issue a patent for a machine which could threaten the livelihood of the hand knitters in a period of severe under-employment which brought, among other things, the creation of the parish relief system in 1601. Lee therefore took nine of his machines to France, where attempts were being made to promote the manufacture of luxury goods such as silk. Unfortunately the assassination of King Henri IV in 1610 ruined his opportunities and Lee died in France at about the same time without having achieved the recognition he sought for his invention. His frames, however, were soon used to establish a French silk knitting industry.

His brother James brought the stocking frame back to London and improved it by adding the fixed or lead sinkers so that a finer fabric could be produced. The use of the frame spread only very slowly: there were fewer than a hundred machines in use by the outbreak of the Civil War. A Company of Framework Knitters was formed in London and incorporated by charter in 1657 and again in 1663. This enabled trade to be regulated by master framework knitters, who took on apprentices and trained them for a period of seven years to become journeymen. Attempts were made to control the quality of products, to keep out foreign competition and to limit entry into the trade by registering apprentices. Some manufacturers of hose objected to such tight controls on their activities and began to leave London and set up their trade in the East Midlands, the original home of the stocking frame. Population had been increasing since the early sixteenth century, so there was a demand from the less wealthy for cheap-

er hose made out of wool, or later cotton, rather than silk. Worsted spinning, using long-staple wool, was already a well-established industry in Leicestershire and silk throwing developed in Derbyshire and Staffordshire during the eighteenth century. The first pair of cotton stockings seems to have been made in Nottingham in 1730, but it was not until improvements in cotton-spinning techniques later in the century enabled a stronger thread to be made that cotton began to supersede silk for lighter hose. The movement of the knitting industry from London continued so that by 1782 nearly 90 per cent of the twenty thousand stocking frames in use in Great Britain were located in the East Midlands and the percentage remained very much the same throughout the nineteenth century although the number of machines increased. Generally, Nottinghamshire specialised in cotton goods, Derbyshire in silk and Leicestershire in worsted.

During the eighteenth century numerous adaptations were made to the stocking frame to increase its versatility. Lee's machine could knit only in stocking stitch, that is plain on the outside and purl on the inside, although machine-made stockings were often embroidered by hand afterwards. A ribbed fabric, that is one plain and one purl stitch in sequence, looked more decorative and had greater elasticity than plain stocking stitch. Frame knitters often laboriously reversed every other stitch by hand to achieve this effect. The *tuck presser,* which was introduced in Nottingham in the middle of the eighteenth century, enabled patterns of zigzags and lozenges to be knitted, but the most important invention was the *Derby rib frame* developed in 1758 by Jedediah Strutt. He first utilised what the contemporary historian and textile manufacturer William Felkin later described as 'a new and great principle, that of applying external means for mechanically selecting and operating upon any individual thread, needle, lever or bar, independent of the rest'. An iron frame was attached to the front of an ordinary stocking frame which contained vertical bearded needles operated in the same way as the horizontal ones, but which entered between them to

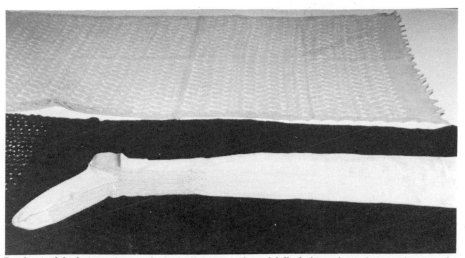

Products of the knitting frame: clocked silk hose made and fully fashioned on a knitting frame and a fine woollen shawl which was made on a special frame equipped with long sinkers and an eyelet attachment to transfer loops from one needle to another.

reverse every other stitch and so create a ribbed fabric. The attachment was often used to knit a ribbed welt for the top of the stocking, a job done by the *topper,* the body of the stocking being knitted in plain stitch by a *middler.* Turning the heel was a complex process involving many alterations to the frame, and often the stocking was *pressed off* or removed from the frame and the loops were picked up again on a separate frame operated by a *footer,* who finished off the stocking.

Other modifications to the frame enabled a wider range of goods to be made. An eyelet attachment enabled loops to be removed from one needle to another, thus creating a pattern of holes in the fabric. This was the beginning of a series of inventions resulting in the development of the machine-made lace trade which became very important in Nottingham during the nineteenth century. The same eyelet attachment, with the addition of deep sinkers to lengthen each stitch, also enabled openwork shawls to be made. In 1795 Crane of Edmonton in Middlesex developed the warp frame by adding warp threads, as on a weaving loom, to the frame and forming looped stitches on these. This type of frame produced a firm but non-elastic fabric which could be made in a variety of patterns and proved particularly suitable for gloves, which became a widespread industry during the early nineteenth century.

The invention of a thread carrier at the end of the eighteenth century saved the knitter laying the thread across the needles by hand and, like Kay's flying shuttle on the weaving loom, enabled wider pieces of fabric to be produced.

These could be cut into shirts, pantaloons, vests and other garments and eventually extended the limited range of goods which could be made on a conventional frame. However, it was also possible to cut stockings from this fabric and seam them up the back, thus producing several stockings from one piece of knitting without the need to adjust the frame for the narrowing and widening necessary to fashion hose. These *cut-ups* or *spurious articles,* as they were known, created great hostility among the knitters of fully fashioned hose since the prices charged for them undercut those of their own products. In the end, however, wide frames were to prove an asset to the industry by enabling it to diversify. Other frames were built to produce several stockings at once, a development made possible by the addition of several slurcocks rather than only one to release the jacks. They became known as 'three-at-once' or 'four-at-once' frames.

By about 1800 the stocking frame had been developed to the limits of its versatility, being able to knit forty distinct types of fabric which could be made into a variety of garments. The way forward lay with the application of power, as in the spinning and weaving industries. The internal organisation of the industry, however, together with an abundant cheap labour force and changes in fashion kept powered machines out of the hosiery trade for a further fifty years.

A 'three-at-once' shawl frame. Notice the three bobbins and the rollers around which the finished portions of the shawl are wound. The springs support the carriage and help the knitter lift it to lock up the sinkers. This machine has now been repaired and stands in Ruddington Museum.

A framework knitter's workshop, from Diderot's 'Encyclopedie' of 1763. Silk knitting developed in France after William Lee's death there in 1614. The knitter has placed his frame close to the window to obtain as much light as possible, while his wife transfers silk from hanks on to bobbins using six-sided winding reels.

THE ORGANISATION OF THE INDUSTRY

The traditional picture of a stocking maker working his frame in his own cottage gives a misleading impression of his independence. It is true that the family worked as a unit, with the man operating the frame, his wife seaming the stockings and, together with the children, winding the yarn on to bobbins for use on the frame. The yarn, however, was not spun at home but obtained in hanks from the warehouse of a merchant, or master hosier, who employed spinners to produce the yarn and who marketed the knitted goods. The knitter was therefore a piece worker, being paid so much a dozen for the hose he produced, and entirely dependent for his wages on the master hosier.

The knitters mostly lived in villages around the towns where the warehouses were situated and so they wasted a great deal of time going into town weekly, usually on Saturday, to take the hose they had made and collect their wages and their new supply of yarn. A knitter from Bulwell, 8 miles (13 km) from Nottingham, told a government commission, appointed in 1844 to enquire into the hosiery industry, that 'I have gone on a Saturday morning, and have got to Nottingham at 9 o'clock exactly, and stopped there till 9 o'clock on a Saturday night, just for the work of those three or four frames.'

Many knitters were compelled to use the services of middlemen such as a *putter out,* who acted as an intermediary between a knitter and the hosier, paying the knitter the prices given by the hosier with some deduction for his own services. Another type of middleman was the *undertaker,* who contracted with a hosier to make a certain quantity of yarn for a given price. Naturally the undertaker would pay lower rates to the knitter than he received from the hosier in order to make a profit for himself. The third class of middleman was the *bag hosier* or *bagman,* who had no agreement with a master hosier but obtained yarn from a number of warehouses and marketed the goods himself. Knitters who worked for bagmen rarely knew the prices being offered by a master hosier and when times were hard they had to put up with the very low rates paid them by the bagman and accept whatever quantity of yarn he allowed them. The middlemen clearly exploited the knitter and not the hosier.

Middlemen soon became employers as well as intermediaries, having knitters working for them rather than directly for a warehouse. Even in the earliest days of the industry, it is doubtful whether many knitters owned their own frames since they represented a considerable capital outlay which many who wanted to enter the industry could not afford. Master hosiers therefore purchased frames and rented them out to knitters, naturally preferring to give work to those dependent on them in this way rather than to those working independent frames. Many knitters who did own their frames were forced to sell them and rent a hosier's frame, and some in desperation paid the rent while continuing to work their own frames. Other people came to realise that purchasing and renting out a frame was a way of securing a good return on their capital outlay. Shopkeepers and other artisans bought frames and often sublet them to middlemen who in turn rented them out to the knitters. As a Nottinghamshire knitter told the 1844 commission, 'there are plenty of bagmen in this town who rent their frames by the year of people we consider do not belong to the trade, such as bakers, brewers and so on; they are rented at 10d a week and charged to us at 1s 6d.'

Frame rent was excessive in relation to the actual cost of a frame. In 1844 narrow frames could be purchased second-hand at from £4 to £8 but were rented out at 1s a week, while wide frames worth £10 to £12 could be rented out at up to 3s a week. Frames had therefore to be rented out for only two or three years to repay the cost and most frames lasted at least twenty years. Maintenance of the frames was supposed to be carried out by the owner, but *framesmiths* complained that the owners did not overhaul their frames very often and the knitters themselves often paid for small repairs to avoid delay. Frame rent also usually had to be paid when the frame was idle either because the knitter was ill or no yarn was available. A Leicester knitter was asked: 'You state that you pay 2s a week frame rent; have you always paid that?' He answered: 'Yes, and always have paid it

Valuable Stocking Frames,

The Property of One Person.

To be peremptorily SOLD by AUCTION,

By GASKILL and PEET,

AT their Sale Room, Long Row, Nottingham, on Monday the 2d Day of June, 1806, at Two o'Clock on that Day, precisely, without Reserve of a single Lot.

No.	G.	W.	Quality.	Where to be viewed.
2 ·	26	16	Cotton,	Mr. Pearson's, Beeston.
4	24	16	Silk,	T. Upton's Mount-st. Nottingham.
5	24	11	Cotton,	Mr. Pearson's, Beeston.
6	30	13	Cotton,	James Porter's, Nottingham.
7	16	16	Rib,	B. Hill's, Gainsburgh.
11	24	13	Cotton,	Mr. Brown's, Drury-hill, Notm.
14	24	12	Cotton,	Mr. Birkin's, Coal-pit-lane, ditto.
15	26	16	Silk,	Mr. Ragg's, Parliament-street, ditto.
16	26	14	Cotton,	Wm. Bingham's, Ruddington.
17	32	16	Cotton,	G. Milner's, Langley.
13	18	16	Rib,	Mr. Brown's, Houghton, near Grantham.
19	24	16	Cotton,	Wm. Shaw's, Ruddington.
20	30	15	Cotton,	G. Brough's, Langley.
21	24	16	Cotton,	T. Muggleston's, Diseworth.
22	24	15	Rib,	Mr. Brotherhood's, Radford
23	25	13	Cotton,	Mr. Norman's, Millstone lane, Nottingham.
24	24	6	Cotton	Mr. Hickling's, Hathern, Leicestershire.
25	24	8	Silk,	Mr. Robinson's, Mount-st. Nottm.
26	26	10	Silk,	Mr. Upton's, Mount-street, ditto.
27	27	7	Cotton,	Mr. Ragg's, Parliament-st. ditto.
28	26	8	ditto	ditto ditto ditto
30	27	17	ditto	ditto ditto ditto
32	30	10	Ditto,	Edward Newton's, Langley.
33	32	28	Ditto,	E. Morrel's, Richmond-st. Ntm.

Buying frames to rent out at a profit was a good investment. The seventy-four frames advertised for sale in the Leicester Journal, 23rd May 1806, are owned by one person but worked in shops scattered through twenty villages in Nottinghamshire and Leicestershire.

whether I have been on full work, or half work, or quarter work, whether sick or well, whether one day little work or no work, or whether there are any circumstances, as there are sometimes, that you cannot do any; the charges have to be paid all the same.'

The hosiers claimed that frame rent was necessary to ensure that only their work was done on their frames, but since a large proportion of the frames were owned by middlemen during the nineteenth century it is more likely that frame rent continued because it was a reliable source of income for the owner. The result was a gross over-production of frames, and therefore the market for knitted goods became glutted in the first half of the nineteenth century and so prices, and therefore wages, declined.

14

As there were more frames than there was available work, employers often *stinted* the knitters, sharing the work around, yet continuing to deduct full frame rent. Knitters also had to pay for needles and oil for the frames. If their wives were unable to undertake seaming the stockings or their children the winding of bobbins, it was their responsibility to get these tasks done by someone else and to pay for them. Between a third and a half of their income was absorbed in charges connected with their work, particularly during the winter, when candles and coal also had to be paid for. Finally, when frames began to be grouped together in shops rather than worked at home, employers often charged *standing* rent for the frames on their premises, and some even went so far as to charge standing for a rented frame in a knitter's own house. As one Nottinghamshire knitter said, 'the master I work for holds seventy-three frames and has no more standing than he can set three frames in, yet he takes, in the shape of standing, 3d for each of those seventy-three frames.'

The many grievances of the framework knitters concerning the organisation of their industry were aired at great length during the 1844 investigation. The Leicester section of the commissioners' report sums up the whole problem: 'While wages remain, as they have done for years past, almost at the minimum of existence to the workman; while custom sanctions, and his defenceless poverty forces him to submit to pay an exorbitant and disproportionate weekly rent for the machine in which he works; while the mode of conducting the business remains in force, which actually prescribes the very limits of labour he shall perform, as subsequently shown in the practice of stinting; and while at any time the employer can, at little sacrifice to himself, lay down his one, or his ten, or his hundred frames — even the rental of the places in which they stand, when at work, being paid by the workmen — there must be great advantages clearly manifested as derivable from any new system of production which shall preponderate over those yielded by the present one.'

The report was right as far as the knitter was concerned. But it was not to the advantage of the hosier or middleman to change a system of production so clearly favourable to him, and it was to be another thirty years before any significant changes were made in the organisation of the hosiery industry.

SOCIAL CONSEQUENCES

'As poor as a stockinger' was a common and regrettably apt saying during the nineteenth century. The organisation of the industry was the main cause of the poverty of the framework knitters but their wage levels were also affected by changes in demand due to disruption of markets by war or by changing fashion. Knitters took part in several of the major upheavals during the nineteenth century, including Luddism and Chartism, but in the end they were forced to rely on self-help and wait for the industry to adapt itself to the changing conditions.

The American colonies were an important market for knitted goods, and therefore the export trade suffered badly during the conflict between Britain and America in the 1760s and 1770s and again between 1811 and 1815. During the first of these periods wages fell rapidly but food prices remained high. The knitters petitioned the House of Commons in 1778 for an Act to fix wage levels, but although a committee was set up to investigate the problem no Act was passed. Trade revived with the end of the War of American Independence, and the wars against France initially stimulated the industry by creating a demand for clothing for the army and navy. However, by 1811, a combination of high taxation, bad harvests, decreasing demand at home because of general poverty and finally the closure of the American market reduced the framework knitters once more to abject poverty. William Cobbett's picture of the knitter quitting his frame at eleven o'clock at night after seventeen or eighteen hours of work, eating his solitary potato and crawling in to sleep among his children who had been

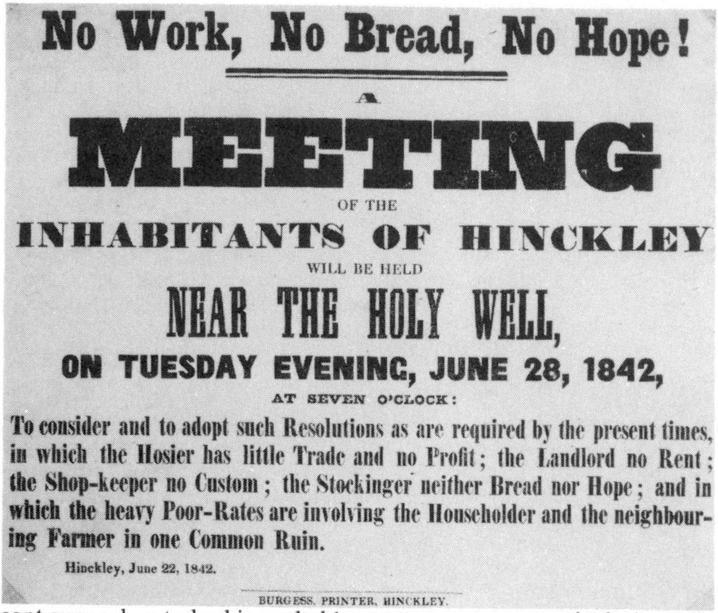

No Work, No Bread, No Hope!

A

MEETING

OF THE

INHABITANTS OF HINCKLEY

WILL BE HELD

NEAR THE HOLY WELL,

ON TUESDAY EVENING, JUNE 28, 1842,

AT SEVEN O'CLOCK:

To consider and to adopt such Resolutions as are required by the present times, in which the Hosier has little Trade and no Profit; the Landlord no Rent; the Shop-keeper no Custom; the Stockinger neither Bread nor Hope; and in which the heavy Poor-Rates are involving the Householder and the neighbouring Farmer in one Common Ruin.

Hinckley, June 22, 1842.

BURGESS, PRINTER, HINCKLEY.

The poverty of framework knitters was a byword during the nineteenth century. Conditions were especially bad in the 1840s; in Hinckley over three thousand people were dependent on parish relief. The following year the knitters petitioned Parliament for a Commission to enquire into the problems of their industry.

sent supperless to bed is probably not too gross an exaggeration of the truth.

Unable to understand the more general causes of their poverty, the framework knitters blamed the manufacture of cut-ups, which the hosiers were producing in response to the demand for cheaper goods. Many frames were broken in a wave of destruction which affected the East Midlands during 1811 and 1812, particularly the wide frames which were now often grouped in shops and therefore particularly vulnerable to the frame breakers. Manufacturers who had reduced wages often had their frames treated in the same way. The combination of resentment over cut-ups, hunger and poverty motivated the frame breakers to act as this report from the Nottingham Journal illustrates: 'A party of armed men, to the number of about twenty, entered the house of Mr Shepherd, in the parish of Stapleford, and demolished four frames, for the making of cut-up work, for stockings; and, not contented with this atrocity, they carried off a flitch of bacon, and stole and took away the children's clothes, two pairs of shoes and other articles.'

The Nottinghamshire frame breakers were particularly well organised, operating in groups and claiming to be under the control of the mythical 'Ned Ludd', whose headquarters was supposedly in Sherwood Forest. Offending employers would receive a threatening letter signed by Ludd, promising to break their frames if certain demands were not met. It is difficult to calculate how many frames were broken in 1811-12 since many reports were exaggerated, but it was probably not more than one thousand of the twenty-five thousand frames being worked in the three East Midland counties. Luddite tactics did have some success in the short term in stabilising wage levels and checking the production of cut-ups, but these improvements were not to be permanent. A bill prohibiting the manufacture of cut-ups passed the Commons in 1812 but was rejected by the Lords; it would have been difficult to enforce, since the wide frames themselves did more good than harm to the industry by enabling it to diversify into the production of knitted goods other than stockings.

Frame breaking became more sporadic after 1812 and the famous attack on Heathcoat's lace factory in Loughborough in 1816 was in many ways a

16

ABOVE: *A timber-framed house in Shepshed, Leicester-shire, which was adapted for framework knitting by adding an extension at the side of the house and inserting two long windows. There are similar windows at the back. Shepshed was dominated by framework knitting: in 1851 well over half its households were engaged in the trade.*

RIGHT: *The Luddites were well organised in Nottingham into frame-breaking gangs. The generous reward offered for information leading to convic-tion indicates how seriously the authorities regarded their activi-ties, particularly in the years 1811-12.*

WHEREAS,

Several EVIL-MINDED PERSONS have assembled together in a riotous Manner, and DESTROYED a NUMBER of

FRAMES,

In different Parts of the Country:

THIS IS

TO GIVE NOTICE,

That any Person who will give Information of any Person or Persons thus wickedly

BREAKING THE FRAMES,

Shall, upon CONVICTION, receive

50 GUINEAS

REWARD.

And any Person who was actively engaged in RIOTING, who will impeach his Accomplices, shall, upon CONVICTION, receive the same Reward, and every Effort made to procure his Pardon.

☞ Information to be given to Messrs. COLDHAM and ENFIELD.

Nottingham, March 26, 1811.

17

postscript to Luddite activity. Like many other hosiery and lace manufacturers, Heathcoat was compelled by the contraction of the market to reduce wages, and his factory was attacked by a group of Nottinghamshire Luddites, who burned the lace and destroyed almost all the fifty-five machines there. One of the gang later turned King's evidence and after a widely publicised trial in Leicester six men were hanged and three transported for life. A similar fate befell several knitters who joined in the Pentrich Revolution in 1817. Fierce penalties, together with the use of special constables and military force to disperse rioters, put an end to Luddism and forced the framework knitters to revert to their previous tactics of association and of petitioning the government. The genuine distress of the knitters did elicit some sympathy: Lord Byron, whose home was in Nottinghamshire, made an impassioned speech in the House of Lords in 1817, pleading on behalf of the Luddites that 'nothing but absolute want could have driven a large, and once honest and industrious, body of the people, into the commission of excesses so hazardous.' But most people in Britain were terrified by the prospect of violence and revolution after what had happened so recently in France, and the *Nottingham Journal* probably expresses the more typical reaction to the events of 1812 to 1817: 'We congratulate the public upon the vigorous proceedings adopted for putting an end to the shameful system of destroying frames . . . In addition to the liberal rewards offered, some of the most active and intelligent officers from Bow Street are now employed, and have been in the adjacent villages during the past week.'

The framework knitting industry did not recover until the introduction of steam-powered frames in the 1870s. As well as the general depression affecting British trade after 1815, changing fashion had severe repercussions on the industry. Dress had become more restrained and there was little demand for fancy hosiery, most knitters being forced into the less well paid plain wrought hose branch of the trade. As one manufacturer said in 1844, 'I used to wear breeches, now I wear pantaloons and I do not need

anything above a 24 gauge; the coarser gauge stocking affords me comfort and that is all that is wanted. I do not want show at all. It is the same with the ladies, they wear boots and long clothes; the stockings are not seen. Whether they have the finest silk stocking or the commonest cut, it would be all the same, except perhaps in the ballroom.'

Wages continued to fall steadily, being between 10 shillings and 15 shillings a week for the average knitter although many in the wrought hose trade earned far less. Attempts in the early 1820s to form relief societies to help the knitters had no long term success, since a slight upturn in trade meant that public sympathy declined and subscriptions ceased to be forthcoming. Many framework knitters joined in Chartist meetings and petitions in the 1830s and 1840s but, as in 1811-12, suffered imprisonment without achieving the satisfaction of their demands. Conditions worsened, as they did in many other industries, in the early 1840s and had become so bad by 1843 that a further petition, signed by twenty-five thousand framework knitters, was sent to the House of Commons asking again for a commission of enquiry. The petition was granted and evidence was taken, as we have seen, during 1844, but once again nothing positive was done. The commissioner, Mr Muggeridge, recognised that the heart of the problem was overmanning in the industry but only made recommendations which the government did not choose, or was unable, to enforce. The evidence given in 1844 does, however, enable us to see at first hand the social conditions of framework knitters in the 1840s. However, the commissioners were enquiring into reasons for distress and therefore perhaps concentrated on the worst cases. Even so, it is clear that appalling conditions were generally being experienced throughout the East Midlands, perhaps more severely in the villages than in the towns, where a greater variety of goods was beginning to be made.

John Thurman of Shepshed, a village near Loughborough, had a wife and seven children and knitted plain wrought hose. He told the commission: 'The boy and me make four dozen of them in a

Half-timbered cottages in Hinckley, Leicestershire. They probably date from the seventeenth century and have more window space than normal contemporary houses. The left-hand end of the cottages is maintained as a small museum by Messrs Atkins, whose large late nineteenth-century factory opposite dwarfs these cottages and emphasises the change in scale which took place within the industry once power was introduced.

week; then I have to pay 2s 3d frame rent for the two frames; then I have to pay 2 shillings for seaming and I have to pay 7½d for needles for the two frames; then I have to pay for candles 4d per week. Then there is oil I have to pay 2d for; then I have the materials to buy towards the frame, wrenches, hammers, keys and everything of that sort. My little boy does the winding, that would be 6d if I was obliged to put anybody else to do it. Then I have coal 1s 3d per week, that is in the summer we do not use as much as that, but in the winter we use fire, that is, for the house and shop and all.'

His income amounted to £1 2s 3d a week and his expenditure on the expenses of his work, his rent and coal came to 9s 7½d. This left the family 12s 8½d a week for food and clothing. Many knitters' families had even less: 3s 6d for a

family of six is listed on several occasions in the 1844 report. John Thurman continued his evidence by saying that: 'The whole nine of us lie in two beds, and for those two beds we have one blanket for both; and it is out of my power, in any shape whatever, to buy any more without my earnings were more. I can positively say, and it is not my wish or principle to state one word of the least untruth, never a week goes by but I have to put my wife to bed for want of food; anybody that could come forward and knew me, would testify to that . . . when I have got my little on a Saturday, I pay every farthing I can, as far as it will go — and then when Monday morning comes I have not got 6d to buy a loaf with and there is nothing in the house. Then whatever few garments we have about us we take them and pledge them into the shop to get a bit of

bread to go on with during the week, as long as it will last; sometimes it lasts till Thursday dinner time, and then we have to go without until Saturday when we get our things again.'

Many other knitters pledged their clothes to obtain food in this way. A Hinckley pawnbroker reckoned he paid out about £70 a week to between six hundred and seven hundred people: 'Friday is the worst; they will bring in small trifling articles, such as are scarcely worth a penny, to enable them to buy a bit of meat or a few trifles for dinner.'

A grocer said that women would pull off their aprons and offer them to him to buy bread for their children. They made great efforts to redeem their clothes on Saturdays so that they could look respectable on Sundays, but many knitters said they could not send their children to Sunday school to learn to read or write because they were ashamed to do so as

they were so badly clothed. Schooling at any other time was an impossibility, as the knitters relied on the income their children could bring in as winders or footers. Some knitters said that they would have liked to apprentice their children to other trades but could not afford the premium demanded, and so their children were forced to work in their own already overcrowded industry.

It is hardly surprising that the amount of parish relief dispensed in the East Midlands increased during the first three decades of the nineteenth century. The New Poor Law of 1834 attempted to make entry into a workhouse the normal means of poor relief and, as was intended, greatly reduced the number of those seeking help. One framework knitter said that he had before now lived on barley bread, without butter or cheese, for two months and never sought a farthing from the parish. As many knitters rented frames from grocers and other shopkeepers, the practice of truck was common, by which wages were paid in goods, often at inflated prices, rather than in cash. Truck was abolished by Act of Parliament in 1831 but the prohibition was impossible to enforce and the practice continued in the framework knitting industry for many years. Attempts were made to set up sick clubs and clothing clubs in many hosiery villages, through which members received assistance in times of need in return for a regular subscription; the funds were often added to by local benefactors. The poorest could not afford the subscription and so help did not reach those most in need, who were often in the end forced into the workhouse. Another means of alleviating distress was the renting out of allotments, on which knitters could at least grow potatoes and vegetables to sustain their families. While frame rent continued, however, knitters were forced to work long hours to earn the money to pay it and so the allotment system was not as effective as it could have been in helping to reduce the glut of knitted goods on the market as well as relieving poverty.

Several attempts were made in the first half of the nineteenth century to organise framework knitters into a trades union, but the scattered nature of the industry made this more difficult to achieve than in other factory-based textile industries. Overmanning in the industry also made knitters unwilling to join a union, knowing that it might prevent their being given work for their frames. Strikes took place on many occasions, but they were not co-ordinated and had little permanent effect. In the end, it was the efforts of the more enlightened hosiers which, together with changes in the organisation of the industry itself, brought about improvement in the life of the stockinger.

HOUSES AND WORKSHOPS

By the middle of the nineteenth century knitting frames were being worked in over 220 parishes in the three East Midland counties, one hundred in Leicestershire, and at least sixty in each of Nottinghamshire and Derbyshire. The majority of the frames stood in the knitters' houses or in shops attached to them, but others were already beginning to be grouped together in separate workshops often called *frameshops*. The late introduction of power into the hosiery industry resulted in the survival of many hand-powered units until well into the twentieth century. The study of surviving buildings can therefore be used, in conjunction with documentary evidence, to provide a detailed picture both of the distribution of the industry and of the life of the framework knitters.

The operation of a knitting frame required close co-ordination between the movements of hands, eyes and feet, and so the knitter needed as much light as possible to fall on his frame. Artificial light could be provided by placing a candle behind a glass globe filled with water, which intensified the light of the single flame. Candles were expensive, and knitters tried to work as much as possible without them, making maximum use of daylight. Large elongated windows and lack of internal walls were the main characteristics of knitters' workshops.

In the earliest days of the industry long windows were inserted into the walls of existing houses where the frame was placed. Such alterations can often be detected in half-timbered buildings where a wooden beam has been cut to allow a window to be inserted or where the house has more windows than would be normal for a house of its period. Careful study of such alterations to buildings is the only way of locating exactly where the stockings were made in the period for which detailed documentary evidence, such as census returns, is not available.

The knitting frame must have been a very cumbersome object to have in a small house and wherever possible knitters preferred to use a separate room for their frames, often building one on to their houses or erecting a separate workshop in the garden or backyard. Workshops were also built by middlemen who could then rent out space for frames as well as the machines themselves. As the industry expanded during the eighteenth and nineteenth centuries, hosiers and others seized upon an opportunity for further profit by building rows of houses incorporating workshops and letting them to knitters at a rent which was by the mid nineteenth century 1s 6d to 2s per week. This was an additional burden to men whose net earnings, after deduction of expenses connected with their work, was rarely more than 10s a week and often much less. As one knitter said in

A terrace of four three-storey cottages with typical long windows front and back on the second floor, where the frames would have been situated.

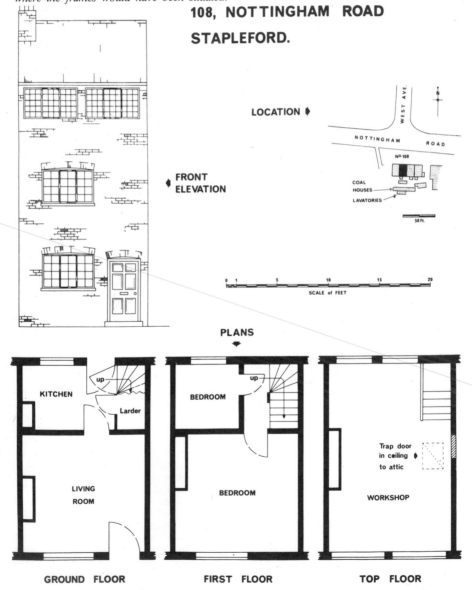

108, NOTTINGHAM ROAD
STAPLEFORD.

FRONT ELEVATION

LOCATION

WEST AVE.

NOTTINGHAM ROAD

Nº 108

COAL HOUSES
LAVATORIES

50 ft.

0 1   5   10   15   20
SCALE of FEET

PLANS

GROUND FLOOR

KITCHEN

up

Larder

LIVING ROOM

FIRST FLOOR

BEDROOM

up

BEDROOM

TOP FLOOR

Trap door in ceiling to attic

WORKSHOP

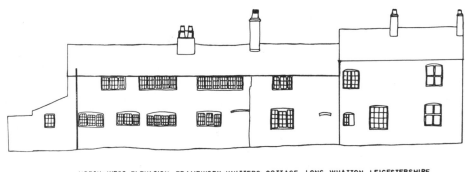

NORTH-WEST ELEVATION, FRAMEWORK KNITTERS COTTAGE, LONG WHATTON, LEICESTERSHIRE.

SCALE: 0 1 3 5 7 metres

A. Patrick.

Extensions to house frames were often added behind houses which fronted village streets, as here in Long Whatton.

1844, 'Every man must take his frame where he can. I myself have a house where I set my own in, and I am obliged to have a house with a shop in it, that costs me extra rent.' A study of the surviving examples of such purpose-built housing suggests that there may have been regional differences in the type of workshops preferred, but as so many have been demolished it is impossible to be certain that this was the case.

The best known type of stockinger's house resembles that built for weaving in Lancashire and Yorkshire or silk manufacture in Macclesfield, Coventry or the Spitalfields area of London. This is of three storeys with a workshop on the top floor, easily identified by its elongated windows. The ground floor contained a living room and kitchen and the first floor usually two bedrooms. The *topshop* was often connected by a door to the one in the next house and may have had attic space above for storage of yarn. Light into the shop was not usually interrupted by other buildings at this level, but the weight of the frame meant that the floor had to be supported by heavy beams and the room was usually floored with a lime mortar mixture. The frames, because of their bulk, were largely erected *in situ* by a framesmith. Three-storey knitters' houses are most common in west Nottinghamshire, south Derbyshire and the northern part of Leicestershire. East of Nottingham and in parts of Leicestershire

rather more examples survive of two-storey houses incorporating a workshop on the ground floor with its elongated windows. The shop floor needed less reinforcement and the parts of the frame could be brought into the house more easily, but unless the house was extended at the back the living space for the family was less than in a three-storey house with a top-floor workshop. The light must also have been less good, particularly if other buildings stood close by.

These houses provided reasonable accommodation by the standards of the time, but their existence must not delude us into thinking that the majority of knitters lived in comparative comfort. Families living in such purpose-built houses often took in lodgers, who added their frames to those of the family and contributed to household costs, but whose presence reduced living space. The 1844 report indicates how large many families were, yet in towns and larger industrial villages frames were crammed into basements, cellars or attics, with the family occupying at the most two rooms elsewhere in the house. Most of these cramped dwellings have been demolished, but some still survive in Nottingham, where a look at the backs of houses can often reveal the characteristic elongated windows. The courts and alleys of the town housed as many, if not more, of the framework knitters than did the purpose-built houses and shops with

23

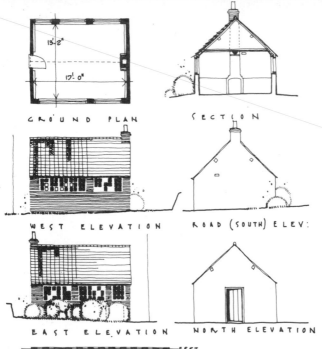

GROUND PLAN

13'-2"

17'-0"

SECTION

WEST ELEVATION

ROAD (SOUTH) ELEV:

EAST ELEVATION

NORTH ELEVATION

0 5 10 15 20 25 FEET

Single-storey workshops with windows on all four sides or the two longer sides are characteristic of the nineteenth-century hosiery industry. Here, Tom Foster is standing in front of his shop in Caythorpe, Nottinghamshire, about the year 1910. It is possible to count at least six frames inside, while a water-filled glass globe hangs by one of the windows to direct light on to the needles. The plans show that the shop was heated by a single grate.

which we tend to associate them.

In Leicestershire the use of the wide frame spread more quickly than in the other two counties, and this may partially account for the separate frameshop being more common than purpose-built housing. Frameshops were much more frequent in Leicester than in Nottingham, where the late enclosure of the open fields around the city meant that land was not available. A Leicester manufacturer told the 1844 commission that there were many shops housing between fifteen and fifty frames in the town and that knitters working in them earned about 2s 6d a week more than those at home since they did not pay frame rent. This was not always the case, as some hosiers still charged frame rent and standing but preferred to concentrate their frames in shops so that they could supervise the quality of the goods produced and ensure that work was done at regular hours. Smaller frameshops were often of one storey only, with windows on all four sides. Larger ones were of two storeys, with rows of continuous windows on at least the two longer sides of the building. Some had windows only on the top floor, where the frames stood to get most of the light, the bottom floor being used for storage. Inside the frames were placed very close together, as was pointed out by a witness giving evidence to the Factory Commission of 1833: 'There were six frames; three on each side. The room measured in height 6 feet 8 inches (2.03 m), in length 13 feet (3.96 m), in breadth 10 feet 6 inches (3.20 m). The frames were wide ones, turning off three or four stockings each at a time. They measured all alike, viz 5 feet (1.52 m) in length placed traversely with relation to the length of the room, height 5 feet (1.52 m), width 3 feet (0.91 m). It will be seen from the above proportions that little more than 6 inches (150 mm) were left for passage between the two rows of frames. I got to the other end of the room with difficulty by stooping and moving sideways, where I found a little boy with a winding machine occupying the only

Part of a row of six single-storey workshops in Earl Shilton, Leicestershire, which were probably built for hosiery in the mid nineteenth century and later utilised for the production of boots and shoes. They stand in the backyards of a terrace of six houses with long windows on the ground floor at the rear, similar to Windles Square in Calverton.

Ruddington frameshop, now a museum. Notice how the frames are placed very closely together, giving each knitter very little room.

space left by an irregularity in the wall. The men sat at their work back to back; there was just space for the necessary motion, but not without touching each other. The room was so close almost to smother one.'

A frameshop of this kind has been preserved as a museum in Ruddington, Nottinghamshire, where the working conditions of the knitters in such shops can be readily appreciated.

Many detached workshops survive in the East Midlands but not all housed frames. Some were used by hosiers to provide space for winding and seaming and finishing of knitted goods, as stockings cut out of knitted fabric had to be seamed and shaped on a leg board.

Towards the end of the nineteenth century when hosiery production became steam-powered and moved into factories, many workshops were taken over by the boot and shoe industry, particularly in the southern part of the area. Other workshops were used for the manufacture of needles and sinkers for the frames, work which also needed good light and so had large windows. It is only by comparing documentary sources with surviving visual evidence that a true picture of the hosiery industry can be recreated, but it is of particular interest because so much evidence survives of a home-based industry of a kind that was superseded much earlier in other kinds of manufacture.

THE HOSIERY FACTORY

The manufacture of knitted goods was the last branch of the textile industry to adapt to mechanical power. Yarn spinning had been done by water power from the 1770s and by steam power from the earliest years of the nineteenth century but as the widespread use of steam-driven knitting frames did not develop until the later years of the nineteenth century, the industry never passed through a water-powered phase.

Experiments with power-driven knitting frames were numerous during the nineteenth century. Marc Isambard Brunel was granted a patent in 1816 for a steam-powered rotary machine, but the problems of the industry at this period presumably prevented its adoption. The idea of a rotary machine was taken up again in the late 1830s since it could operate faster than a flat machine which involved a series of discontinuous movements. More rotaries were adopted after Matthew Townshend invented the latch needle in 1847. On this type of needle the barb was operated by the yarn itself as the loops passed over it in a similar manner to a modern rug hook. The presser bar to close the needle beards was no longer necessary and so rotary machines using latch needles were simpler to operate. Power-driven hosiery factories using rotaries were opened in

the middle decades of the nineteenth century but the machines could knit only circular fabric which was not shaped in any way and so it was used for cut-ups. Fashioned articles were still made on the hand frame and so inventors concentrated on the problem of widening and narrowing fabric automatically. Arthur Paget of Loughborough and Luke Barton of Hyson Green, Nottingham, both solved the problem of narrowing fabric in the same year, 1857, Paget producing a one-off machine and Barton a wide frame producing several lengths at once. Another Loughborough manufacturer, William Cotton, first solved the widening problem and then in 1864 received a patent for automatic narrowing and widening using a fine-gauge frame. His machine still made use of Lee's spring bearded needles, but they were placed vertically in the frame and the sinkers horizontally, with the bar to which the sinkers were attached acting as a presser to close the needle beards. The apparatus for transferring loops to narrow and widen fabric hung above the row of needles and could be adjusted at the turn of a screw. Cotton's machine was soon widely adopted in the hosiery trade and he established a separate factory which was producing a hundred machines a year by the late 1870s.

The days of the hand frame were therefore numbered, but only changes in the organisation of the industry could permit the full exploitation of the new machines. Felkin had suggested in 1844 that only the concentration of frames in shops and adapting them to steam power would improve conditions in the industry, but this was difficult to achieve while hosiers and middlemen still had a vested interest in renting out frames. Attempts had been made during the 1850s to abolish this rent but without success. In the 1870s a parliamentary commission was appointed to enquire into the persistence of truck in mining areas, and this was extended into hosiery areas, where it was claimed that frame rent was a peculiar kind of truck. Several manufacturers gave evidence, including A. J. Mundella, a Nottingham manufacturer who was also Member of Parliament for Sheffield. He

The town of Hinckley in Leicestershire probably preserves the typical industrial landscape of steam-powered hosiery production better than anywhere else in the East Midlands. The factories are mostly small; the building on the left preserves an elaborate chimney and a wall-mounted crane for hoisting yarn to the top floor. The Gothic windows in the factory below are picked out in yellow brick.

William Cotton invented the basic knitting machine movements used in modern equipment. He moved to this factory in Pinfold Gate, Loughborough, in the 1880s. The different buildings are identified in the engraving and include a forge, needle and sinker departments and several erecting shops.

said that steam frames would eventually do away with frame rent altogether, but on surviving hand frames it should be a matter of negotiation, not a legal deduction. The commission, however, decided on outright abolition, which was done by Act of Parliament in 1874. This undoubtedly hastened the demise of the hand frame, but the process was speeded up even further by the Education Acts of the 1870s, which extended the practice of elementary education, making schooling compulsory until the age of ten. Knitters were therefore prevented from using their children as bobbin winders and seamers, and the family unit of production was irrevocably broken.

Factories developed extensively during the 1880s and 1890s. Many were small, built by bag hosiers who had previously employed knitters working their frames in scattered houses and shops. Others were large, employing thousands of hands. The early factories can often be recognised by the domestic style of their windows, and these were many in number since light was as important in the

factory as in the workshop. Most had large chimneys for the boilers which provided steam for the machines. Carved and moulded bricks were widely used on buildings at this period, and many of these late nineteenth-century factories are very pleasing in appearance.

Factory production brought about a radical change in the nature of the work force employed in the hosiery industry. Power-driven machines did not need the application of human muscle and so could be looked after by women rather than men. The number of men employed in hosiery was halved in the final decades of the nineteenth century, but fortunately the problem of unemployment was not as great as it might have been because new industries provided alternative work. Some men went into the boot and shoe industry, particularly in Leicestershire, where it was expanding rapidly in the years around 1900. Engineering absorbed many others, particularly those in the ancillary trades of framesmith and sinker maker, where they had learnt the necessary skills. The result was a new prosper-

I. and R. Morley were among the largest of Nottingham's hosiery manufacturers. This photograph was taken about 1900 and shows their factory, built in 1877 and little altered over a hundred years later.

ity for the East Midlands with both men and women finding adequate employment. Both public buildings and housing of the late nineteenth and early twentieth centuries in the area bear solid witness to this prosperity and contrast sharply with the dire distress of the framework knitters as reported in the 1844 commission report.

During the twentieth century the industry has had to adapt itself further on many occasions, particularly to the use of synthetic yarns as well as to changes in fashion far more frequent than in the nineteenth century. However, the world recession has affected the textile industry as it has many others, with imports of cheaply produced knitted fabrics making times hard for the hosiery industry. Many factories have closed and, where they

have not been demolished, are now in multiple occupation by small firms producing goods other than hosiery. Once again, unemployment is a serious problem in the East Midlands and technical improvements are not likely to be the solution.

However, a few East Midland firms still use hand frames to make shawls and fancy knitwear and they have adapted powered machines to produce similar fabrics. Their order books are full, particularly for the export market, and their knitted fabrics are used in the latest fashions in Paris and New York. Four hundred years after William Lee invented the knitting frame, goods produced on very similar machines still have a part to play in the world market.

30

FURTHER READING

Felkin, W. *A History of the Machine-Wrought Hosiery and Lace Manufactures.* Originally published 1867; centenary edition with an introduction by S. D. Chapman, David and Charles, 1967.

Grass, M. and Grass, A. *Stockings for a Queen : The Life of the Reverend William Lee.* Heinemann, 1967.

Henson, G. *History of the Framework Knitters.* First published 1831; reprint with an introduction by S. D. Chapman, David and Charles, 1970.

Palmer, M. (editor). *Leicestershire Archaeology — The Present State of Knowledge. Volume 3: Industrial Archaeology.* Leicestershire Museums, Art Galleries and Records Service, 1983.

Smith, D. *The Industrial Archaeology of the East Midlands.* David and Charles, 1965.

Wells, F. A. *The British Hosiery and Knitwear Industry : Its History and Organisation.* Revised edition 1972, George Allen and Unwin.

There are also very useful articles in the *Victoria County History* of both Leicestershire and Nottinghamshire, and in the journals *Textile History* and *East Midland Geographer,* and the *Bulletin of the Leicestershire Industrial History Society* and the *Nottinghamshire Industrial Archaeology Society Journal.* The East Midlands Collection at Nottingham University Library and the Library at HATRA, the Hosiery and Allied Trades Research Association, 7 Gregory Boulevard, Nottingham, telephone Nottingham (0602) 623311, have good collections of books, journals and pamphlets on framework knitting.

The label used by G. H. Hurt and Son, who produce fine lace-patterned knitwear both on hand frames and on powered frames adapted for the purpose.

PLACES TO VISIT

MUSEUMS

Calverton Museum, Calverton, Nottingham. Telephone: Nottingham (0602) 652886. A small museum containing relics of the industry, including a hand frame, open by appointment.

Leicestershire Museum of Technology, Abbey Pumping Station, Corporation Road, Leicester. Telephone: Leicester (0533) 661330. Gallery of knitting frames and an archive collection.

Newarke Houses Museum, The Newarke, Leicester. Telephone: Leicester (0533) 554100 extension 220. Knitted articles and some machines.

Nottingham Industrial Museum, Courtyard Buildings, Wollaton Park, Nottingham NG8 2AE. Telephone: Nottingham (0602) 284602. Knitting and lace machinery.

Ruddington Framework Knitters' Museum, Chapel Street, Ruddington, Nottingham. Telephone: Nottingham (0602) 213287 or 211858. Open by appointment. A unique complex containing hand frames *in situ,* together with the living quarters of the knitters.

White Gate Farm Museum, Wigston, Leicester. Open by appointment with the owner, Duncan Lucas. An interesting display of the needles used in the knitting industry.

INDUSTRIAL ARCHAEOLOGY

The best surviving complex of buildings is Windles Square in Calverton, Nottinghamshire (National Grid Reference SK 621491). Examples of early frameshops can be seen in the main street of Sutton Bonington (SK 503256), Hinckley (SP 428943) and Shepshed (SK 483196). Purpose-built three-storey houses with topshops survive in Stapleford (SK 506279) and workshops can be seen in Bonsall (SK 274581), Wigston (SP 604987) and Kegworth (SK 488264). Attractive early factories still survive in Leicester and Hinckley.

The reader is referred to the gazetteers in the works by M. Palmer and D. Smith (see Further Reading, page 31), to the East Midlands Tourist Board publication *Industrial Archaeology in the East Midlands* and to the revised editions of Pevsner's *Buildings of England* series for *Leicestershire, Derbyshire* and *Nottinghamshire.*

WORKING UNITS

Several firms still use hand frames for the manufacture of shawls. A good example is G. H. Hurt and Son, 65 High Road, Chilwell, Nottingham; telephone: Nottingham (0602) 254080. There are several small Leicester firms, about which information can be obtained from Leicestershire Museum of Technology, where hand frames are demonstrated on certain days. The frames are also occasionally worked at Ruddington Framework Knitters' Museum.

ACKNOWLEDGEMENTS

The author would like to thank John Heath for comments on the text and Eric Starling, Norton Collier, Mary Ball, Bob Bracegirdle, John Severn, Amber Patrick and Professor David Smith for help with illustrations. Peta Lewis of Ruddington Framework Knitters' Shops Preservation Trust patiently demonstrated their hand frames and photographs were taken by David Palmer and Angus Bentley. Other illustrations are acknowledged as follows: Institute of British Geographers, page 2; diagrams by David Eveleigh, pages 5 and 6; Loughborough Public Library, page 7; Victoria and Albert Museum, page 8 (bottom); Leicestershire Record Office, page 16; Ruddington Museum, page 17 (bottom); Nottinghamshire County Library Service, page 20; David and Charles, page 22.